AI Risk Management & Compliance

Preventing Lawsuits, Fines & Reputational Damage

By Joe Correa

Published by Live Stronger Faster

This book is for educational and informational purposes only. The author and publisher are not engaged in rendering legal, financial, or other professional advice. Readers should consult a qualified professional before making any financial decisions.

First Edition

Table of Contents

Overview

Artificial intelligence has now reached a point where it no longer operates quietly in the background of software systems—it actively makes decisions that affect money, health, liberty, reputation, and even life itself. Algorithms approve mortgages, deny insurance, flag fraud, predict crime, decide who gets hired, and determine which patients receive care first. This enormous power has created a new kind of corporate risk, one that no legal department, compliance officer, or executive team can afford to ignore. AI risk is not theoretical. It is already generating lawsuits, regulatory investigations, billion-dollar fines, destroyed brands, and executive resignations. This book exists because the organizations that survive the AI era will not be the ones with the most advanced algorithms, but the ones that manage algorithmic risk better than everyone else.

For decades, companies have mastered financial risk, legal risk, cybersecurity risk, and operational risk. But AI introduces a completely new category: algorithmic risk. Unlike traditional software, AI systems learn, evolve, and make probabilistic decisions. They are influenced by training data, hidden correlations, feedback loops, and human behavior in ways that even their creators cannot always predict. This creates a dangerous illusion of control—companies deploy models believing they are deterministic tools, when in reality they behave more like complex organisms. When those systems fail, discriminate, hallucinate, or cause harm, regulators and courts do not care that the algorithm was "learning." The organization that deployed it is held responsible.

The age of unregulated AI experimentation is ending. Governments around the world are now imposing binding obligations on companies that deploy AI. The European Union's AI Act, U.S. consumer protection laws, discrimination statutes, financial regulations, healthcare laws, and privacy frameworks all now intersect with AI systems. Every automated decision that touches a human being can now become a compliance event. Every model output can become legal evidence. Every dataset can become a liability. AI risk management is no longer optional; it is becoming as fundamental as financial controls and cybersecurity programs.

What makes AI uniquely dangerous from a compliance standpoint is that it scales harm at machine speed. A biased loan officer might discriminate against dozens of people. A biased AI model can discriminate against millions before anyone notices. A faulty medical judgment by a doctor affects one patient. A faulty AI diagnostic system affects entire hospital networks. A human mistake is isolated. An AI mistake is exponential. This is why regulators are moving quickly, lawsuits are exploding, and insurance companies are raising alarms. AI risk is not just another IT issue—it is now one of the most powerful enterprise-level threats that organizations face.

This book is designed for leaders, compliance teams, legal departments, risk officers, insurers, regulators, founders, and engineers who must now operate in this new reality. You will not find vague ethics discussions here. You will find practical frameworks for preventing legal exposure, regulatory violations, and brand-destroying AI failures. We will show how risk emerges inside machine learning systems, how it travels through data pipelines and vendors, and how it explodes into lawsuits when left unmanaged. We will also show how organizations can build defensible AI programs that regulators trust, insurers underwrite, and courts respect.

One of the greatest myths in the AI industry is that responsibility lies with the machine. It does not. Every algorithm is ultimately an extension of corporate decision-making. When an AI denies a mortgage, approves a medical procedure, flags a suspect, or rejects a job candidate, the organization is making that decision—just through code instead of a human. The law sees no meaningful difference. The company that trained, deployed, or relied on that model carries full responsibility. That is why governance, auditability, documentation, and oversight are becoming just as important as model accuracy.

Modern compliance is no longer about ticking boxes—it is about proving control. Regulators and courts increasingly demand that companies demonstrate how decisions were made, why they were made, and whether they were fair, lawful, and safe. AI systems that cannot explain their outputs or produce audit trails are legal nightmares. This book will show you how to build governance structures that allow your organization to demonstrate control over even the most complex machine learning models.

AI risk also extends far beyond your own code. Vendors, third-party APIs, cloud models, open-source datasets, and outsourced AI services all introduce hidden liabilities. When something goes wrong, regulators will not accept "a vendor did it" as an excuse. If you deployed the system, you own the risk. We will examine how vendor risk, model sourcing, data licensing, and outsourced AI systems must be managed as part of a unified compliance strategy.

Another major shift occurring right now is the involvement of insurance and financial regulators. Cyber insurance once forced companies to adopt security standards. Now AI insurance and professional liability policies are beginning to require model governance, validation, monitoring, and incident response plans. If your organization cannot prove responsible AI controls, it may soon be uninsurable. That means one catastrophic AI failure could wipe out the company. Risk management is no longer just about avoiding fines—it is about survival.

This book also addresses a brutal truth: most organizations do not even know what AI systems they are running. Models get deployed by marketing, HR, finance, customer support, and product teams without centralized oversight. Shadow AI proliferates. Data flows across borders. Decisions are made without documentation. When regulators or litigators come knocking, companies scramble to reconstruct what their systems did. By then, it is already too late. We will show how to inventory, classify, and govern AI across the enterprise before crisis strikes.

AI compliance is not about slowing innovation—it is about making innovation sustainable. Organizations that master risk management will be able to deploy AI faster, safer, and with greater confidence. They will win regulatory trust, customer loyalty, and investor confidence. Those who ignore compliance will find themselves trapped in lawsuits, blocked by regulators, and shunned by partners. The winners of the AI economy will be those who can prove their systems are not just powerful, but lawful, fair, and controlled.

Throughout this book, you will learn how to build AI risk frameworks that align with emerging global regulations, how to create model governance structures that executives and boards can trust, how to design compliance checklists that engineers can actually follow, and how to prepare for audits, incidents, and legal challenges before they happen. This is the playbook for turning AI from a dangerous liability into a defensible, insurable, enterprise-grade asset.

AI is rewriting the rules of business, law, and accountability. Organizations that treat it casually will pay the price. Organizations that master risk will dominate their industries. The future belongs not to the companies with the most powerful algorithms, but to the ones that control them the best. That is what this book will teach you to do.

Chapter 1

What Is AI Risk in Our Lives

AI risk is the total exposure an organization faces when artificial intelligence systems make, influence, or automate decisions that affect people, money, safety, or legal rights. Unlike traditional software, which follows static rules, AI systems operate probabilistically. They predict outcomes rather than execute instructions. This makes them powerful, but also inherently unpredictable. When an AI model makes a decision, it is not "running code" in the traditional sense—it is applying mathematical patterns learned from historical data. Those patterns often contain bias, error, outdated assumptions, and hidden correlations that no human ever explicitly approved. This means every AI output carries legal, ethical, financial, and reputational risk.

The first dimension of AI risk is legal risk. Whenever an AI system touches employment, credit, housing, healthcare, education, insurance, law enforcement, or financial services, it becomes subject to existing civil rights, consumer protection, and regulatory laws. If an algorithm disproportionately harms a protected group, the organization that deployed it can be sued for discrimination, even if no one intended to discriminate. Courts do not accept "the model did it" as a defense. They look at the outcome, not the intent. AI systems now generate massive volumes of legally actionable decisions, turning every model into a potential lawsuit engine if not properly governed.

The second major category is regulatory risk. Governments worldwide are rapidly introducing AI-specific laws, including the EU AI Act, algorithmic accountability rules, and sector-specific guidance for healthcare, finance, and surveillance. These laws require companies to classify AI systems by risk level, document how models are trained, validate their performance, and monitor them continuously. Noncompliance can result in enormous fines, forced shutdowns, and bans on using certain technologies. AI risk is therefore not just about whether your system works, but whether you can prove to regulators that it works safely, fairly, and legally.

Operational risk is another hidden threat. AI systems do not just fail once—they drift over time. As markets change, user behavior evolves, and data shifts, models become less accurate and more biased. A system that was compliant at launch can become dangerous months later without anyone noticing. This is known as model drift, and it has caused financial institutions, healthcare providers, and tech platforms to make increasingly wrong decisions while believing everything was still under control. Without monitoring systems and governance frameworks, organizations often discover problems only after harm has already occurred.

Reputational risk may be the most damaging of all. When AI systems go wrong, the public reaction is often brutal. Stories of biased algorithms, wrongful arrests, denied benefits, or misdiagnoses spread quickly. Trust evaporates. Customers leave. Investors panic. Regulators investigate. Even if a company survives the legal fallout, the brand damage can last for years. AI failures are perceived not as technical glitches, but as moral failures. They suggest that a company values efficiency over humanity, which is deadly in a trust-driven economy.

There is also financial risk embedded in AI systems. Incorrect predictions can lead to bad loans, false fraud flags, rejected customers, and mispriced insurance. These errors scale instantly across thousands or millions of users. Traditional mistakes cost thousands. AI mistakes cost millions. Worse, many organizations do not even realize how much money they are losing because they do not measure model performance beyond surface-level accuracy. True AI risk includes hidden revenue leakage, regulatory capital penalties, and increased insurance premiums.

Data risk is another foundational element. AI systems are only as safe as the data they consume. If data is illegally collected, biased, outdated, or incomplete, the model trained on it becomes legally toxic. Privacy violations, consent failures, and unauthorized data usage can all trigger massive penalties. Synthetic data, third-party datasets, and scraped information create additional exposure that many companies never audit. When regulators investigate, data lineage becomes one of the first things they demand to see.

Vendor risk is now one of the fastest-growing categories of AI exposure. Most organizations rely on external models, APIs, or data sources. If those vendors violate the law, leak data, or deploy biased systems, the organization using them can still be held responsible. This creates a dangerous blind spot, where companies think risk has been outsourced when it has actually been multiplied.

AI risk also includes existential risk to business continuity. A single catastrophic failure—such as wrongful arrests, denied healthcare, or mass discrimination—can trigger injunctions, lawsuits, and regulatory bans that shut down operations overnight. This is why modern risk management treats AI as a critical system on par with financial reporting and cybersecurity.

In reality, AI risk is not a single threat. It is a network of legal, technical, ethical, financial, and reputational dangers that feed into each other. A biased dataset leads to discriminatory outcomes. Those outcomes lead to lawsuits. Lawsuits lead to regulatory scrutiny. Regulatory scrutiny leads to fines and shutdowns. And all of it happens at machine speed. Understanding this chain reaction is the first step to controlling it.

Organizations that understand AI risk do not avoid AI—they master it. They build governance, monitoring, documentation, and accountability into every model. They treat algorithms like high-risk employees who must be supervised, audited, and trained continuously. This chapter establishes the foundation for that mindset. AI is not just technology. It is a source of power, and all power must be governed.

The Algorithm That Nearly Destroyed Orion Bank

Orion Bank was once one of the most respected financial institutions in the country. For over a century, it had built its reputation on careful lending, community trust, and conservative risk management. But when fintech startups began eating into its market share, Orion's executives panicked. They needed speed, scale, and automation. That is when they approved a powerful AI-driven lending platform designed to approve home equity lines of credit in seconds.

The sales pitch was irresistible: higher approval rates, lower costs, and zero human bottlenecks.

At first, the system worked beautifully. Loan volume exploded. Profits soared. Executives celebrated the algorithm as the future of banking. What no one noticed was that the model had been trained on decades of historical lending data—data that reflected past discrimination, redlining, and unequal access to credit. The algorithm learned those patterns perfectly. It quietly began approving far fewer loans for certain neighborhoods, certain income profiles, and certain demographic groups.

No alarms went off. The compliance team never saw a red flag. From a pure profit standpoint, everything looked fine. But outside the glass towers of Orion Bank, people began to notice. Borrowers who had always qualified were suddenly being rejected. Small business owners were being denied credit without explanation. Community organizations started filing complaints.

Then the lawsuits came.

Civil rights groups accused Orion Bank of running a discriminatory black-box lending system. Regulators demanded documentation. Journalists demanded transparency. The bank could not explain how its AI made decisions, only that it did. That was not good enough. Investigators demanded training data, decision logs, and model audits. Orion had none of them. The fines were staggering. The reputational damage was worse. Customers fled. Investors sued. Executives were forced to testify before Congress. The AI that had once been celebrated became the symbol of corporate negligence.

Inside the company, panic spread. Engineers scrambled to retrace how the model worked. Lawyers tried to limit liability. Compliance officers realized they had no governance framework for AI at all. They had trusted the machine, but never controlled it.

Orion Bank survived, but barely. The lesson was burned into every boardroom in the industry: AI does not just create efficiency. It creates risk at scale. And if you do not manage that risk, it will manage you.

From that day forward, every major financial institution rewrote its playbook. Algorithms were no longer treated like software—they were treated like powerful, dangerous decision-makers. And the age of AI risk management had truly begun.

Chapter 2

Model Governance to Decide Who Is Responsible

Model governance is the system of rules, roles, processes, and controls that ensure artificial intelligence models behave in ways that are lawful, ethical, predictable, and defensible. In traditional software development, governance focuses on code changes and version control. In AI systems, governance must go much deeper because models learn from data, adapt over time, and produce probabilistic outcomes that no one can fully predict. Model governance exists to answer one critical question: who is responsible when an algorithm makes a decision, and how can that decision be justified to regulators, courts, customers, and executives?

At its core, model governance creates accountability. Without it, AI becomes a corporate black box where no one truly owns the decisions being made. Marketing deploys a model. Engineering builds it. Legal hears about it only when something goes wrong. Compliance never sees it. This fragmentation is the root cause of most AI disasters. Proper governance assigns clear ownership at every stage of the model lifecycle, from design and training to deployment, monitoring, and retirement. Someone must be responsible for the model's performance, fairness, compliance, and safety at all times.

A mature governance framework begins with model inventory. An organization cannot govern what it does not know exists. Every AI system must be cataloged, classified by risk level, and documented. High-risk models—those affecting credit, employment, healthcare, legal rights, or financial outcomes—must be subject to enhanced oversight. This classification is now required under laws such as the EU AI Act and emerging U.S. regulations. Even low-risk models must still be tracked because risk can change as models are repurposed or connected to new data.

Model governance also requires formal approval processes. No AI system should be deployed into production without review by compliance, legal, and risk teams. This is not to slow innovation, but to ensure that risks are understood before harm occurs. Governance boards or AI ethics committees review use cases, training data sources, performance metrics, and compliance implications. If a model cannot be explained, audited, or justified, it should not be released.

Documentation is another pillar of governance. Every model must have a record explaining how it was built, what data was used, what assumptions were made, and what risks were identified. This documentation becomes legal armor. When regulators or courts demand answers, organizations must be able to produce clear evidence of due diligence. Without documentation, even a harmless model can become a legal liability.

Monitoring is where governance becomes dynamic. AI systems cannot be "set and forget." Performance, bias, accuracy, and drift must be continuously measured. A model that was compliant at launch can become dangerous months later as data changes. Governance frameworks require automated monitoring systems that trigger alerts, reviews, and retraining when thresholds are breached. This turns AI into a controllable system instead of a runaway process.

Model governance also includes escalation and shutdown authority. If an AI system starts causing harm, someone must have the power to pause or disable it immediately. Kill switches, rollback mechanisms, and incident response protocols are essential. Without them, companies are forced to watch damage accumulate while lawyers debate what to do.

Vendor and third-party models must be governed just as strictly as internal ones. Contracts should require audit rights, compliance guarantees, and transparency. If a vendor refuses to provide documentation or testing results, that is a risk signal. Governance does not stop at your firewall.

Finally, model governance must reach the board level. Executives and directors are increasingly being held personally accountable for algorithmic failures. They must understand what AI systems the company runs, what risks they carry, and how those risks are controlled. Governance transforms AI from a hidden technical asset into a visible, manageable business system.

Without governance, AI becomes a legal and ethical minefield. With governance, it becomes a powerful, trusted tool. That is the difference between companies that collapse under algorithmic risk and those that thrive.

The Model No One Owned

Virex Health was a fast-growing medical technology company that used AI to predict which patients were most likely to develop complications after surgery. Hospitals loved it. The system helped doctors allocate resources and save lives. But inside Virex, no one could say who actually owned the model.

Engineering built it. Product sold it. Marketing advertised it. Legal assumed it was safe. Compliance never reviewed it. No one monitored it. Then one hospital noticed something strange. Patients from one demographic group were consistently being flagged as "low risk" even when they had serious warning signs. Several of those patients later suffered severe complications. Families demanded answers. Lawyers demanded data.

Virex scrambled. Engineers could not explain why the model behaved that way. The training data was old. The model had drifted. No one had monitored it. No one had documented it. There was no approval record, no audit trail, no governance board.

When regulators arrived, they did not ask who wrote the code. They asked who was responsible.

The board froze. No one could answer.

The company's stock collapsed. Hospitals canceled contracts. Lawsuits piled up. All because a powerful AI system had been allowed to operate without ownership, oversight, or control.

In the aftermath, Virex rebuilt from the ground up. They created model inventories, governance boards, monitoring systems, and kill switches. Every algorithm now had an owner. Every decision had documentation.

They learned the hard way what every company must now understand: an algorithm without governance is not innovation. It is a liability waiting to explode.

Chapter 3

Compliance Checklists Between AI Governance and Real-World Operational Control

Compliance checklists turn regulatory requirements, legal obligations, and ethical standards into actionable steps that teams can actually follow. Without checklists, AI compliance exists only on paper. With them, it becomes embedded in product development, deployment, and monitoring. In a world where algorithms make thousands of decisions per second, checklists ensure that every one of those decisions rests on a foundation of due diligence.

The first purpose of an AI compliance checklist is risk identification. Before a model is trained or deployed, organizations must determine whether it falls into a high-risk category. Does it affect credit, employment, healthcare, law enforcement, or financial outcomes? Does it use biometric data, personal information, or behavioral tracking? These questions are not academic. They determine which laws apply, which approvals are required, and what level of documentation must exist. A checklist forces teams to confront these questions early, before a model becomes operational and dangerous.

The second function is data compliance. AI systems depend on vast datasets, but not all data is legal to use. A proper checklist verifies data sources, consent, ownership rights, privacy compliance, and security protections. It ensures that personal information is handled according to GDPR, HIPAA, CCPA, and other frameworks. It also confirms that datasets are representative and free from known bias risks. Without this step, even a technically perfect model can become legally toxic.

Model testing is another critical area covered by compliance checklists. Before deployment, models must be evaluated for accuracy, fairness, stability, and robustness. This includes testing against protected groups, stress-testing edge cases, and validating that outputs align with legal and ethical expectations. A checklist ensures that testing is not skipped under deadline pressure. It makes compliance part of the engineering workflow rather than an afterthought.

Documentation is where compliance becomes defensible. Checklists require that training data, model architecture, testing results, and decision logic are recorded in a way that auditors and regulators can understand. This creates an evidentiary trail that proves the organization acted responsibly. When something goes wrong, documentation can be the difference between a manageable investigation and catastrophic liability.

Deployment controls are another essential checklist area. Who approved the model? What version is live? What safeguards exist? Is there a rollback plan? Checklists force teams to answer these questions before pushing code into production. They prevent unauthorized or experimental models from reaching customers.

Post-deployment monitoring is equally important. Compliance does not end at launch. Checklists require ongoing measurement of accuracy, bias, drift, and incidents. They ensure that someone is watching the model and that problems trigger investigations and corrective actions. Without this step, organizations operate blind.

Finally, incident response is built into compliance checklists. When an AI system causes harm, there must be a predefined process for stopping it, investigating it, notifying regulators, and compensating affected users. Checklists transform chaos into controlled response.

Compliance checklists do not exist to slow innovation. They exist to make innovation survivable. In a regulated, high-risk world, the companies that win will be the ones who can prove, step by step, that they built AI responsibly.

The Checklist That Saved Atlas Credit

Atlas Credit was rolling out a new AI-powered loan approval system designed to outpace every competitor. The engineers were confident. The sales team was ecstatic. Launch day was scheduled.

Then the compliance officer stopped it.

She pulled out a single document: the AI compliance checklist.

The model had not been tested for bias. The data source was unclear. No one had documented consent. There was no rollback plan. The checklist said no.

Executives were furious. Delays meant lost revenue. But they relented.

Two weeks later, during bias testing, the team discovered that the model rejected a huge percentage of self-employed applicants—even when their financials were strong. The training data had been skewed by outdated underwriting rules.

If the model had gone live, Atlas would have faced massive discrimination lawsuits.

Instead, they fixed it.

When regulators later reviewed Atlas's AI program, the checklist became their shield. Every step was documented. Every risk was addressed. Every control was in place.

Competitors were fined and shut down. Atlas kept growing.

In the end, the checklist that almost killed the launch saved the company.

Chapter 4

Why Audit Trails Are the Backbone of AI Accountability

Audit trails are the digital records that show exactly how an algorithm was built, how it was trained, what data it used, which version was deployed, what decisions it made, and why those decisions occurred. In traditional business systems, audit trails have always existed for money, contracts, and security. In the age of artificial intelligence, they must also exist for algorithms. Without audit trails, an AI system is legally indefensible, ethically opaque, and operationally dangerous.

When regulators, courts, or investigators examine an AI system, they do not ask whether it is innovative. They ask whether it is traceable. They want to know who approved it, what assumptions were embedded into it, what data influenced its outputs, and how it changed over time. If those answers cannot be produced, the organization is presumed negligent. An audit trail transforms an AI model from a mysterious black box into a documented decision system that can be reviewed, tested, and challenged.

At the most basic level, an AI audit trail records the lineage of a model. This includes when it was created, which team built it, what data was used, what features were engineered, and what objectives it was designed to optimize. It also includes version history, so that when a model is updated or retrained, there is a record of what changed and why. This is critical because many legal disputes hinge not on what a model does today, but what it did at a specific point in the past.

Audit trails also capture decision logs. Every time an AI system produces an output that affects a person or a business outcome, that event should be recorded. This allows organizations to reconstruct exactly how and why a decision was made. In credit, hiring, healthcare, and insurance, these logs become legal evidence. Without them, organizations cannot defend themselves against claims of discrimination, negligence, or regulatory violations.

Data lineage is another critical element. Organizations must be able to prove where data came from, how it was processed, whether consent was obtained, and how long it was retained. This protects against privacy violations, intellectual property disputes, and regulatory penalties. Audit trails connect models to the data that powers them, making invisible risks visible.

Modern AI systems also require performance logs. Accuracy, bias metrics, drift indicators, and error rates must be tracked continuously. These logs show whether a model is behaving as expected or slowly becoming dangerous. When harm occurs, these records demonstrate whether the organization acted responsibly or ignored warning signs.

Audit trails are not just technical artifacts. They are legal shields. They allow companies to show regulators that they exercised due care, followed best practices, and maintained control. They also give executives the visibility they need to manage risk proactively.

Without audit trails, AI systems become ungovernable. With them, they become auditable, defensible, and trustworthy.

The Logs That Proved the Truth

NovaSure Insurance used AI to decide which claims to approve and which to investigate for fraud. It saved millions of dollars—until one policyholder accused the system of unfairly denying her medical claim.

The lawsuit was brutal. The woman's lawyers demanded to know exactly why the algorithm rejected her case. They claimed discrimination. They demanded proof.

NovaSure's legal team turned to the audit trail.

Every step was there. The data used. The model version. The exact probability score. The rules that triggered the review. The human override that followed. It showed that the decision was based on objective risk factors, not bias.

Regulators reviewed the logs and agreed.

The case was dismissed.

Competitors without audit trails were not so lucky. They paid millions in fines and settlements.

NovaSure learned what every AI-powered business must now know: in the age of algorithms, if it isn't logged, it didn't happen—and if you can't prove what happened, you will lose.

create a 7 page chapter 5 in paragragh format and then a 7 page story with a story title (and make them really 7 pages long!)

Chapter 5

AI Vendor Risk: One Of The Most Underestimated Dangers

Very few companies today build all of their AI systems from scratch. Instead, they rely on cloud platforms, foundation models, data brokers, annotation services, SaaS tools, APIs, and pre-trained algorithms supplied by third parties. Each of those vendors introduces not just technical dependency, but legal, ethical, financial, and reputational risk. When an AI system causes harm, regulators and courts do not ask who built it. They ask who deployed it. That means every organization that uses third-party AI inherits the full liability of that vendor's mistakes, even if it had no visibility into how the system was created.

The first layer of vendor risk is data legality. Many AI providers train models on massive datasets scraped from the internet, purchased from brokers, or sourced from unknown origins. If that data includes copyrighted material, personal information, medical records, or biometric data collected without consent, every company using that model is exposed to lawsuits and regulatory penalties. Organizations must therefore demand proof of lawful data sourcing, documented consent, and compliance with privacy regulations such as

GDPR, HIPAA, and CCPA. If a vendor cannot demonstrate where its data came from and how it was obtained, the safest assumption is that it is legally contaminated.

The second layer is bias and discrimination risk. Vendors often claim their models are fair, but few provide detailed testing across protected classes. A model trained on biased historical data will replicate and amplify that bias. If an organization uses that model in hiring, lending, insurance, healthcare, or public services, it can become the defendant in civil rights lawsuits. Vendor contracts must therefore require bias testing, fairness metrics, and access to evaluation results. Blind trust in vendor claims is not a compliance strategy—it is a lawsuit waiting to happen.

Security risk is another critical concern. AI vendors often have access to sensitive customer data, internal business information, and proprietary models. If a vendor suffers a breach, that data may be exposed, stolen, or used to train other models. Organizations remain responsible for protecting their customers even when the breach occurs at a supplier. This means vendor risk management must include cybersecurity audits, encryption requirements, access controls, and breach notification obligations. Operational risk also flows through vendors. If a critical AI service fails, is shut down by regulators, or changes its terms of service, an organization's core operations may collapse overnight. Companies that build products or workflows around third-party AI without contingency plans are effectively outsourcing their business continuity. Vendor governance must therefore include redundancy, exit strategies, and the ability to migrate models or data if needed.

Transparency is one of the most important but hardest requirements. Many AI vendors treat their models as trade secrets, refusing to disclose training methods, data sources, or decision logic. While intellectual property deserves protection, complete opacity is incompatible with regulatory compliance. Organizations must be able to explain how their AI works. If a vendor cannot support explainability, auditability, and regulatory review, it should not be used in high-risk contexts.

Contracts are the legal backbone of vendor risk control. AI vendor agreements must include warranties of legal compliance, rights to audit, obligations to provide documentation, indemnification for regulatory penalties, and requirements to cooperate with investigations. Traditional software contracts are not sufficient. AI creates new categories of risk that must be explicitly allocated.

Ongoing monitoring is also essential. A vendor that was compliant at onboarding may become risky as it updates its models, changes its data sources, or expands into new markets. Organizations must continuously review vendor performance, audit results, and regulatory status. Vendor risk is not static—it evolves with every model update.

Ultimately, vendor risk is enterprise risk. Companies that fail to govern their AI suppliers are gambling with their legal standing, their brand, and their survival. True AI compliance does not end at the edge of your network. It extends through every API call, every dataset, and every algorithm you did not build yourself but still rely on.

The Vendor That Almost Bankrupted Helix Systems

Helix Systems was a fast-growing financial technology firm that specialized in automated small-business loans. To stay ahead of competitors, they licensed a powerful AI underwriting engine from a popular Silicon Valley startup. The vendor promised lightning-fast approvals, better risk predictions, and full regulatory compliance. Helix signed the contract and went live in less than a month.

At first, everything looked perfect. Loan volume tripled. Defaults dropped. Investors poured in more capital. Helix's CEO was hailed as a visionary for embracing AI so aggressively.

Then the complaints began.

Small business owners from minority-owned neighborhoods were being rejected at alarming rates. Journalists started investigating. Civil rights groups filed complaints with regulators. Helix's executives demanded answers from the vendor.

The vendor had none.

Their model had been trained on decades of historical banking data that reflected discrimination, redlining, and unequal access to capital. Worse, some of the training data had been purchased from a data broker who had illegally collected personal financial records. Regulators launched investigations into both the vendor and Helix.

Helix tried to claim it was the vendor's fault. The regulators didn't care. Helix deployed the system. Helix denied the loans. Helix was liable.

The fines were devastating. Lawsuits followed. Investors fled. The company's valuation collapsed by eighty percent in six months.

Only after the crisis did Helix realize the truth: they had outsourced their intelligence without governing their risk. They had trusted a vendor instead of controlling one.

When Helix finally rebuilt, they demanded audit rights, bias testing, data provenance, and compliance guarantees from every AI supplier. They never again treated a vendor's algorithm as someone else's responsibility.

They survived—but only because they learned what nearly destroyed them: in the age of AI, your vendor's mistakes are your own.

Chapter 6

AI Model Validation in Real-World Conditions

Model validation is the process of proving that an artificial intelligence system does what it claims to do, does not do what it should not do, and remains reliable under real-world conditions. In traditional software, validation means checking that the code runs without errors. In AI, validation is far more complex, because models do not follow fixed rules—they learn patterns from data, and those patterns can be wrong, biased, unstable, or dangerous. A model that looks impressive in development can become catastrophic in production. Validation is what stands between experimentation and legally defensible deployment.

The primary goal of model validation is not simply accuracy, but trustworthiness. A highly accurate model that discriminates, drifts, or behaves unpredictably is more dangerous than a mediocre one that is stable and explainable. Regulators, courts, and compliance officers care far more about whether a system is safe, fair, and controlled than whether it is cutting-edge. Validation therefore examines how a model behaves across different populations, conditions, and edge cases, not just whether it achieves a high performance score on a test dataset.

A proper validation program begins with data validation. If the data is flawed, the model will be flawed. Organizations must confirm that training data is complete, representative, legally sourced, and free from known bias patterns. Missing data, over-representation of certain groups, or outdated records can all distort a model's behavior. Validation requires statistical analysis of data distributions, correlation testing, and bias detection before any model is even trained.

Once the model is built, performance validation begins. This involves testing the model on data it has never seen before and measuring not only accuracy, but false positives, false negatives, stability, and error patterns. In regulated industries, this testing must be segmented across protected classes to ensure that one group is not disproportionately harmed. A model that performs well overall but poorly for a specific population is legally and ethically unacceptable.

Stress testing is another critical layer. Models must be exposed to extreme, unusual, and adversarial inputs to see how they behave under pressure. Real-world environments are messy, and users will always behave in unexpected ways. Validation seeks to identify failure modes before customers or regulators do. This is especially important in healthcare, finance, and law enforcement, where errors can destroy lives. Explainability validation is also required. Organizations must ensure that they can understand, at least at a high level, why a model makes the decisions it does. Black-box systems that cannot be explained are extremely difficult to defend in court. Validation includes checking whether the model produces interpretable outputs, whether decision factors can be traced, and whether explanations are consistent.

Model validation is not a one-time event. Drift occurs when data changes, markets shift, or user behavior evolves. A validated model can become invalid within months. Continuous validation programs monitor performance and fairness over time, triggering retraining or shutdowns when thresholds are crossed. This is what transforms AI from a fragile experiment into a controlled enterprise system.

Ultimately, validation is the foundation of AI risk management. Without it, organizations are guessing. With it, they can prove that their systems deserve to be trusted.

The Model That Almost Killed a Hospital

Starlight Medical Center had just deployed a new AI system to predict which patients were at risk of internal bleeding after surgery. The vendor promised life-saving accuracy. The hospital rushed it into production. Within weeks, doctors noticed something terrifying. Several patients flagged as "low risk" began crashing without warning. Nurses questioned the system. Administrators dismissed them. The algorithm said everything was fine.

One surgeon refused to accept it. She demanded a validation audit.

The data was old. The model had never been tested on elderly patients. The hospital's patient population had changed, but the algorithm had not. It was blind to the very people it was supposed to protect.

When regulators arrived, they found no validation records, no stress tests, and no bias analysis. The hospital nearly lost its license.

The system was shut down. A new, validated model replaced it.

Lives were saved.

From that day on, Starlight treated AI like a medical device: tested, validated, and monitored constantly. Because in medicine—and in AI—trust without validation is fatal.

Chapter 7

Monitoring Systems in an AI-powered Organization

Monitoring systems are the nervous system of an AI-powered organization. They provide continuous awareness of how models are behaving in the real world after deployment, turning invisible algorithmic activity into measurable, actionable signals. Without monitoring, an AI system is effectively operating blind. It may appear to function correctly while quietly drifting into bias, inaccuracy, or regulatory noncompliance. With monitoring, organizations can detect problems early, intervene before harm occurs, and prove to regulators that they maintain ongoing control over their algorithms.

The need for monitoring arises from a fundamental truth about machine learning: models change even when their code does not. As user behavior shifts, markets evolve, and new data flows into a system, the statistical environment that a model operates in moves away from the conditions under which it was trained. This phenomenon, known as model drift, can slowly degrade accuracy and fairness without any obvious alarms. A credit model may begin rejecting good borrowers. A medical model may misclassify new disease variants. A fraud system may miss emerging scams. Monitoring systems exist to reveal these changes before they cause harm.

Effective AI monitoring begins with defining what "normal" looks like. Organizations must establish baseline performance metrics for accuracy, bias, false positives, false negatives, and stability. These baselines become the reference points against which all future behavior is compared. When metrics deviate beyond approved thresholds, the system should trigger alerts, reviews, or automatic interventions. This turns AI from an unpredictable black box into a controlled process that can be supervised just like any other critical system.

Monitoring must also include fairness and compliance indicators. It is not enough to track overall accuracy. Organizations must measure how different groups are affected by the model's decisions. Disparities across gender, race, age, income, or other protected characteristics can emerge over time even if the model was fair at launch. Continuous fairness monitoring allows companies to detect discriminatory patterns early and correct them before lawsuits or regulatory action occur.

Another essential component of monitoring is anomaly detection. AI systems can behave in unexpected ways when they encounter unusual data, malicious inputs, or system failures. Monitoring tools must identify spikes, drops, or strange patterns in outputs that indicate something has gone wrong. These anomalies may signal data poisoning attacks, technical failures, or misuse of the system. Early detection can prevent cascading damage.

Monitoring systems also serve a legal and regulatory function. Many AI laws now require ongoing oversight rather than one-time approval. Regulators expect organizations to prove that they are watching their models, measuring their impact, and responding to problems. Logs, dashboards, and reports generated by monitoring systems become part of the organization's compliance evidence. Without them, companies cannot demonstrate that they are exercising due care.

Automation plays a crucial role in effective monitoring. Human review alone cannot keep up with the speed and scale of modern AI. Automated tools must collect metrics, analyze trends, and trigger alerts in real time. Human teams then investigate and take action. This hybrid approach ensures both speed and judgment.

Monitoring also supports continuous improvement. By analyzing how models perform in the real world, organizations can identify weaknesses, retrain models, and refine their systems. This creates a feedback loop that improves quality while reducing risk.

In the end, monitoring systems are what make AI governable. They transform models from static artifacts into living systems that can be supervised, corrected, and trusted. Without monitoring, AI is a gamble. With monitoring, it becomes a managed, compliant, and sustainable asset.

The Alert That Saved Meridian Finance

Meridian Finance used an AI system to approve thousands of personal loans every hour. The model had been carefully validated before launch, and everything looked perfect.

Then one night, a silent change began.

A new wave of applicants flooded the system after a viral social media campaign. Their financial profiles were unlike anything the model had seen before. The algorithm began making strange decisions—approving risky loans and rejecting safe ones.

No one noticed at first.

But Meridian had built something most companies did not: a real-time monitoring system. At 2:14 a.m., an alert went off. False positive rates were spiking. Fairness metrics were drifting. The system flagged a potential compliance risk.

Engineers woke up. Compliance officers logged in. They saw the problem and shut the model down before millions of dollars were lost.

A manual review caught the bad approvals. Customers were protected. Regulators were never notified because no harm occurred.

Weeks later, a competitor without monitoring collapsed under a wave of bad AI decisions.

Meridian learned the truth: in the age of AI, survival belongs not to the smartest model, but to the one that is watched the closest.

Chapter 8

Incident Response Under Real Pressure

Incident response is the moment when AI governance is tested under real pressure. It is not enough to have policies, validation, and monitoring if an organization cannot act quickly and decisively when an AI system causes harm. In the world of artificial intelligence, incidents do not unfold slowly. They spread at digital speed, impacting thousands or millions of people before anyone even realizes something has gone wrong. A biased decision engine, a hallucinating legal model, or a faulty medical AI can create catastrophic legal and human consequences in hours. Incident response is the discipline that turns chaos into controlled action.

The first principle of AI incident response is early detection. Monitoring systems, fairness dashboards, anomaly detection tools, and customer complaints all serve as signals that something may be wrong. Organizations must treat these signals seriously. Many AI disasters begin with small warning signs that are ignored because performance metrics still look good. Effective incident response requires a culture where any potential harm trigger is escalated immediately. Once an incident is suspected, the next step is containment. This may mean pausing a model, disabling an API, switching to a fallback system, or forcing human review. Speed matters. Every minute a faulty AI continues to operate multiplies liability. Organizations must have pre-authorized shutdown procedures that do not require endless approvals. Kill switches, rollback capabilities, and isolation mechanisms should be built into every high-risk AI deployment.

Investigation follows containment. Teams must determine what happened, which users were affected, what data was involved, and whether laws or policies were violated. Audit trails, decision logs, and monitoring data become essential. This forensic process must be rigorous, because regulators and courts will later examine it in detail. A sloppy investigation can be as damaging as the original failure.

Notification is another critical component. Many regulations require organizations to inform regulators, customers, or partners when certain types of AI incidents occur, especially when personal data or civil rights are involved. Transparency, when handled properly, can reduce penalties and preserve trust. Cover-ups almost always make things worse.

Remediation is where responsibility becomes visible. Affected users may need to be compensated, decisions reversed, or records corrected. Models may need to be retrained or redesigned. Vendors may need to be replaced. Incident response is not just about stopping harm—it is about making things right.

Finally, lessons learned must feed back into governance. Every incident should result in improved controls, better monitoring, and stronger validation. This is how organizations become more resilient over time.

In AI, failure is inevitable. Catastrophe is optional. Incident response is what makes the difference.

The Night the Algorithm Was Stopped

Clearview Legal used AI to analyze contracts for risk. One evening, a junior lawyer noticed something strange. The system was approving agreements that should have been flagged as dangerous.

He reported it.

Within minutes, the AI incident response team activated. The model was paused. Logs were pulled. They discovered a recent update had caused the system to misinterpret key legal clauses.

Hundreds of contracts had been reviewed incorrectly.

Because the team acted quickly, none were executed. Clients were notified. Regulators were never involved.

A rival firm without an incident response program lost millions when its AI made the same mistake.

Clearview survived because it had prepared for failure.

In AI, speed saves lives—and companies.

Chapter 9

Insurance & Liability in AI Governance

Insurance and liability are rapidly becoming the financial backbone of AI governance. As artificial intelligence systems take on roles once performed by licensed professionals, banks, doctors, analysts, and law-enforcement officers, the legal system has begun to treat algorithms not as software but as decision-making agents. Every automated decision that harms a person now carries the same legal weight as a human mistake. That shift has forced insurers, regulators, and courts to rethink who is responsible when an AI system causes damage. The answer, increasingly, is simple: the organization that deployed it.

Traditional business insurance was built for physical accidents, employee errors, and cybersecurity breaches. AI creates an entirely new class of risk—algorithmic harm. A biased hiring model can generate class-action discrimination claims. A medical AI can cause wrongful death. A lending model can trigger regulatory enforcement. A facial recognition system can lead to false arrests. None of these risks fit neatly into existing insurance categories, which is why insurers are now creating new AI-specific coverage and rewriting professional liability policies to include algorithmic behavior.

One of the most dangerous misconceptions in the AI industry is that using third-party models transfers liability. It does not. If a hospital uses an AI diagnostic tool, the hospital is responsible. If a bank uses a vendor's underwriting model, the bank is responsible. Courts and regulators care about who relied on the system, not who coded it. This makes insurance one of the last lines of defense against catastrophic financial exposure.

AI insurance is now beginning to mirror cyber insurance in its evolution. In the early days, cyber policies were easy to obtain and required few controls. After major breaches, insurers demanded security standards, audits, and compliance programs. AI insurance is following the same path. Insurers now require proof of governance, validation, monitoring, audit trails, and incident response before they will underwrite AI risk. Companies without mature AI risk programs are increasingly uninsurable.

Liability also extends to executives and board members. Regulators are beginning to argue that failing to govern AI is a breach of fiduciary duty. Directors who approve dangerous AI deployments without oversight may face personal liability. This makes AI risk not just a technical or legal issue, but a corporate governance issue. Organizations must therefore treat insurance not as a fallback, but as part of their compliance strategy. Policies should be reviewed for AI exclusions, coverage limits, notification requirements, and cooperation clauses. Vendor contracts should include indemnification and proof of insurance. Models should be deployed only when their risk profile is insurable.

In the AI era, uninsurable systems are unviable systems. Risk that cannot be transferred or absorbed will eventually destroy the business. Insurance forces discipline, documentation, and accountability. It turns AI from a reckless gamble into a financially manageable asset.

The Claim That Shook Ironclad Insurance

Ironclad Insurance had always been conservative. They insured factories, hospitals, and banks—but when their own AI underwriting system denied coverage to a woman whose home later burned down, everything changed.

The woman sued. She claimed the AI had misclassified her property and unfairly raised her premium beyond what she could pay. Without insurance, she lost everything.

The court demanded answers.

Ironclad had no audit trail. No validation. No fairness testing. The algorithm was a black box.

The verdict was brutal.

Ironclad paid millions. Their reinsurers pulled coverage. Their stock collapsed.

Only after the disaster did Ironclad rebuild with proper AI governance, validation, and insurance.

They learned too late that in the age of algorithms, liability is automatic—and protection must be planned in advance.

Chapter 10

AI Compliance Programs Inside An Organization

An AI compliance program is the operating system of responsible artificial intelligence inside an organization. It transforms abstract ethics, legal requirements, and risk management principles into day-to-day business reality. Without a formal compliance program, even the best-intentioned organizations will eventually lose control of their AI systems, because there is no structure to enforce accountability, no framework to manage risk, and no mechanism to prove lawful behavior when regulators or courts demand evidence. In the modern regulatory environment, simply having good technology is no longer enough. Companies must be able to demonstrate that their artificial intelligence is governed, monitored, and controlled as rigorously as their finances or their safety systems.

At its foundation, an AI compliance program defines roles and responsibilities. Someone must own AI risk. Someone must approve new models. Someone must monitor ongoing performance. Someone must respond when things go wrong. In organizations without clear ownership, AI becomes scattered across departments, deployed by marketing, human resources, finance, and engineering without any central oversight. This fragmentation is the root cause of most algorithmic disasters. A compliance program creates a single chain of accountability that runs from the boardroom to the codebase.

Policy is the second pillar. An AI compliance program formalizes what the organization allows and forbids. These policies define which use cases are permitted, which data sources are acceptable, how models must be tested, how long data can be retained, and when human oversight is required. Policies turn regulatory obligations into internal rules that employees can follow. Without them, compliance becomes guesswork, and guesswork becomes liability.

Training is equally essential. Most AI failures are not caused by malicious intent, but by ignorance. Engineers may not understand discrimination law. Product managers may not understand data privacy. Sales teams may not understand the limits of what an algorithm can promise. A compliance program ensures that everyone who touches AI understands the risks, the rules, and the consequences of getting them wrong.

Operational controls are where compliance becomes real. These include approval workflows, documentation requirements, model inventories, audit trails, validation procedures, monitoring systems, and incident response plans. Together, these controls ensure that no AI system can be deployed or operated outside of governance. They create friction in the right places—forcing people to think before they release powerful algorithms into the world.

Auditing and reporting complete the loop. An AI compliance program must regularly test itself. Internal audits verify that controls are being followed. External audits provide credibility with regulators, insurers, and partners. Reports to executives and boards ensure that leadership understands the organization's AI risk posture. Compliance is not a one-time achievement. It is a continuous process.

Finally, an effective compliance program evolves. As laws change, technology advances, and new risks emerge, policies and controls must be updated. Organizations that treat compliance as a static document will fail. Those that treat it as a living system will thrive.

In the AI era, trust is a competitive advantage. A strong compliance program is how that trust is built, maintained, and proven.

The Company That Was Ready

When regulators announced a surprise investigation into AI systems used in financial services, panic swept through the industry. Banks scrambled to gather documentation. Fintech firms shut down models. Lawyers flooded inboxes.

Except for one company.

Aurora Financial had spent two years building a comprehensive AI compliance program. Every model had an owner. Every dataset had documentation. Every decision had an audit trail. Every system was monitored. Every incident had a response plan.

When regulators arrived, Aurora didn't scramble. They opened their compliance dashboard.

Model inventories were produced in minutes. Bias testing reports were handed over. Audit logs showed every decision the AI had ever made. Training records proved employees knew the rules. Incident drills demonstrated preparedness.

The investigation ended quickly.

While competitors paid fines and lost customer trust, Aurora gained new clients who wanted a safe, compliant partner.

Aurora didn't win because it had the smartest AI. It won because it had the best governance.

And in the age of artificial intelligence, governance is power.

Chapter 11

The Future of AI Risk

The future of AI risk will not be defined by technology alone, but by how societies, governments, corporations, and individuals choose to control that technology. Artificial intelligence is evolving faster than any regulatory system in history, and this growing gap between innovation and governance is creating unprecedented levels of uncertainty. Models are becoming larger, more autonomous, and more deeply embedded in everyday life. They will soon manage infrastructure, diagnose disease, approve credit, operate vehicles, recommend prison sentences, and negotiate contracts. As these systems become more powerful, the cost of failure will rise exponentially. A small error in a large system can ripple across entire economies.

One of the most important shifts already underway is the movement from reactive enforcement to proactive risk management. Regulators are no longer waiting for disasters to occur before acting. Instead, they are demanding that organizations identify, assess, and mitigate AI risks before harm happens. This mirrors the evolution of financial and safety regulation, where companies must demonstrate controls before they are allowed to operate. In the future, deploying high-risk AI without a formal risk management framework will be treated as negligence.

Another major trend is the global convergence of AI regulation. While laws will differ by region, core principles are emerging everywhere: transparency, accountability, fairness, security, and human oversight. Companies that build their AI governance around these principles will be able to operate across borders. Those that do not will find themselves locked out of markets. Compliance will become a competitive advantage rather than a burden.

Insurance and capital markets will also play a powerful role. Investors and insurers are already beginning to evaluate AI risk the same way they evaluate cybersecurity and financial controls. Companies with weak AI governance will face higher premiums, higher borrowing costs, and lower valuations. In extreme cases, they may become uninvestable. This financial pressure will force even reluctant organizations to take AI risk seriously.

Technology itself will become part of the solution. AI will be used to monitor AI, detect bias, flag anomalies, and predict failures before they occur. This creates a self-regulating ecosystem where risk is managed continuously rather than episodically. However, this also introduces new layers of complexity, as the systems designed to control AI must themselves be governed.

Human responsibility will remain at the center. No matter how advanced AI becomes, legal and moral accountability will always rest with people. Boards, executives, engineers, and regulators will all be judged by how well they control the systems they unleash. The future of AI risk is therefore the future of corporate governance.

Ultimately, the organizations that survive and thrive in the AI era will not be those that move fastest, but those that move wisely. Risk management is not the enemy of innovation. It is the foundation that makes innovation sustainable.

The Last System Standing

By 2035, nearly every major corporation relied on autonomous AI systems to run their operations. Banks used algorithms to approve loans. Cities used them to manage traffic. Hospitals used them to allocate care. Most companies raced to deploy the most powerful models, believing that speed was the key to survival.

One company took a different path.

Echelon Industries built its empire on something most competitors ignored: AI risk governance. Every system was monitored. Every model was validated. Every decision was logged. Every failure had a response plan.

Then the crisis came.

A global AI vendor released a flawed update that corrupted millions of systems worldwide. Banks mispriced risk. Hospitals misallocated resources. Governments shut down services. Lawsuits exploded.

Echelon was affected too—but its monitoring systems detected the anomaly within minutes. Its incident response team isolated the problem. Its governance framework activated kill switches and fallback systems. While competitors spiraled into chaos, Echelon kept operating.

When the dust settled, hundreds of companies were bankrupt. Echelon stood alone.

Not because it had the best AI—but because it had the best control over it.

In the future, that difference will decide who survives.

Chapter 12

Building a Resilient AI Organization

Building a resilient AI organization means designing a company that can survive, adapt, and thrive even when artificial intelligence systems fail, change, or create unexpected consequences. In the early days of AI adoption, companies focused almost exclusively on speed, automation, and cost savings. They treated models as tools that would eliminate friction and replace human judgment. But as AI systems have become more powerful, their failures have become more expensive. Resilience is now the defining characteristic of successful AI-driven enterprises. It is not about preventing every error, but about being prepared for them.

Resilience begins with mindset. Organizations must accept that AI systems are probabilistic, not deterministic. They will make mistakes. They will drift. They will encounter situations their designers never anticipated. A resilient organization does not panic when this happens. It has already built structures to detect, contain, and correct problems. This mindset must come from leadership. Boards and executives must understand that AI risk is a permanent condition, not a temporary problem to be solved once. Structural resilience comes from distributed oversight. No single team should own all AI decisions. Instead, organizations must create cross-functional governance that includes engineering, legal, compliance, risk, and business leaders. This ensures that technical, legal, and ethical perspectives are applied to every model. It also prevents blind spots, where one department unknowingly creates enormous risk for the entire company.

Technical resilience is built through redundancy and fallback systems. High-risk AI deployments should never be the sole decision-maker. Human-in-the-loop systems, backup models, and manual override processes ensure that when something goes wrong, operations can continue safely. This is especially critical in healthcare, finance, and public services, where interruptions can cause real harm.

Data resilience is equally important. Organizations must protect the integrity, security, and quality of the data that feeds their models. Data breaches, poisoning attacks, and quality degradation can all cripple AI systems. Robust data governance, encryption, access controls, and continuous quality checks are essential.

Cultural resilience may be the hardest to achieve. Employees must feel empowered to question AI outputs, report anomalies, and escalate concerns without fear. Many AI failures happen because people assume the machine must be right. A resilient organization trains its workforce to treat AI as a tool, not an authority.

Finally, resilience is reinforced through continuous learning. Every incident, near-miss, or regulatory change should improve the organization's systems. Resilience is not static. It is a living capability that grows stronger over time.

In a world where AI will continue to evolve and surprise us, resilience is the ultimate form of risk management.

The Company That Refused to Break

When the global supply chain AI crash hit, it didn't start with a bang. It started with a glitch.

One shipping algorithm began misrouting cargo. Then another followed. Within hours, ports were clogged, warehouses overflowed, and factories shut down. Billions of dollars evaporated.

Most companies were helpless. Their operations depended entirely on automated systems they barely understood.

One company, Atlas Logistics, was different.

Years earlier, Atlas had built its AI with resilience in mind. Every routing model had a backup. Every decision could be overridden. Every data stream was monitored. Every employee was trained to question the machine.

When the glitch spread, Atlas detected it within minutes. They switched to their fallback systems. Human teams took control. Operations slowed—but they did not stop.

Competitors collapsed.

Governments asked Atlas for help.

Atlas survived not because it had perfect AI, but because it had built an organization strong enough to handle imperfection.

And in the age of intelligent machines, that is what real strength looks like.

Final Thoughts

AI Risk Management & Compliance

Artificial intelligence is no longer something organizations can treat as experimental technology. It is now infrastructure. It decides who gets hired, who gets approved, who gets monitored, who gets treated, and who gets trusted. When a system has that much power, it inevitably becomes a source of risk. But risk, when understood and managed correctly, does not destroy organizations — it makes them stronger. That is the central lesson of this book. AI does not have to be feared, but it must be governed.

Throughout this book, you have seen how every stage of the AI lifecycle introduces potential exposure: from data collection and model training to deployment, monitoring, vendor relationships, and insurance. These are not theoretical risks. They are already producing regulatory crackdowns, billion-dollar lawsuits, brand collapses, and leadership failures. Organizations that ignore AI risk are not being bold — they are being reckless. And recklessness does not survive long in a world where algorithms shape human lives. What separates the organizations that will dominate the AI era from those that will collapse is not who adopts AI first, but who adopts it responsibly. Responsible AI is not slow. It is stable. It scales because it can be trusted. Regulators allow it. Customers accept it. Investors support it. Insurers underwrite it. That is what compliance really means — not constraint, but legitimacy.

AI risk management is not a defensive posture. It is a strategic advantage. Companies that understand their models, control their vendors, monitor their systems, and prepare for incidents can deploy AI faster and with greater confidence than those operating blindly. When competitors are forced to shut down systems after scandals, compliant companies keep running. When lawsuits cripple ungoverned firms, disciplined organizations expand.

We are entering an era where algorithms will be judged not just by their performance, but by their accountability. The ability to explain, audit, monitor, and correct AI will become as important as speed or accuracy. This book has shown you how to build those capabilities — not as abstract ideals, but as operational systems.

The future of business belongs to organizations that can prove they deserve to wield intelligent machines. Trust will be the ultimate currency of the AI economy. Those who earn it will thrive. Those who ignore it will disappear. AI will continue to change the world. But only those who govern it will control their destiny.

www.ingramcontent.com/pod-product-compliance
Ingram Content Group UK Ltd.
Pitfield, Milton Keynes, MK11 3LW, UK
UKHW020155290926
15471UKWH00005B/884

9 798295 567094